Kerry,
a Teenage Mother

Kerry,
a Teenage Mother

Maggi Aitkens

Photographs by Rob Levine

Lerner Publications Company / Minneapolis

Library of Congress Cataloging-in-Publication Data

Aitkens, Maggi.
    Kerry, a teenage mother / by Maggi Aitkens ; photographs by Rob
Levine.
      p. cm.
    Includes bibliographical references.
    ISBN 0-8225-2556-9
    1. Teenage mothers—United States—Case studies—Juvenile
literature. I. Title.
HQ759.4.A35 1994
362.83′92—dc20   94-897
                                                CIP
                                                 AC

Manufactured in the United States of America
1 2 3 4 5 6 I/JR 99 98 97 96 95 94

To my sister, Mary Anne

Kerry stands at the window in her second-floor apartment, balancing her 15-month-old daughter, Vanessa, on her left hip. Vanessa squirms and tugs on her mother's long black hair. Kerry gazes out the window as she tries to untangle the child's fingers from her hair.

After a minute, she moves to set Vanessa down on the floor. "No!" Vanessa screams.

Kerry murmurs a few quieting words and shifts the heavy child to her other hip. "Who would have thought that things would turn out this way?" she says to herself, thinking back to all that had happened in the past two years, ever since she learned, at age 17, that she was pregnant.

C'mon, we have to get you to day care by 9:00," Kerry says to Vanessa. She quickly whisks the baby's curly, shiny black hair into a ponytail. Vanessa runs up and down the hallway that separates the living room from the bedroom where Kerry, Vanessa, and Kerry's boyfriend, Bill, sleep—Vanessa in a crib and Kerry and Bill on a mattress on the floor.

Kerry chases Vanessa with a wet rag and wipes her face and arms, then sets her free again. Although Vanessa is just over a year old, she's quite steady on her feet and, as Kerry points out, very independent and demanding.

Next Kerry turns her attention to packing all the things her daughter will need for the day—a bottle of juice, diapers, a change of clothes in case she gets dirty, and a car seat. Today Kerry is getting a ride to the day-care center, which is located about a mile away. Sometimes, when the weather is warm, Kerry walks there, carrying Vanessa and all of her stuff. Most days, however, she and Vanessa take the bus, hoping, especially in winter, that it comes quickly, before they get too cold.

This day is warm and sunny, and Vanessa wears a new sundress that her aunt sent from New York. The bright yellow dress shows off Vanessa's large brown eyes and beautiful light brown skin, which she inherited from her mother, who is American Indian, Puerto Rican, and Irish, and her father, Calvin, who is black.

Vanessa has never met her father. One month before she was born, Calvin was arrested for selling drugs and has been in prison ever since. When Kerry first met Calvin, she didn't know he was dealing drugs. In fact, she didn't find out until about a year and a half later, when she moved in with him. Although she was several months pregnant, she knew she didn't want that kind of life for herself and her baby. She decided to end the relationship.

"It's kind of funny," she says. "You meet a guy and think you know him, and then you end up finding out that he's totally different from what you thought."

While in prison, Calvin doesn't pay child support. (When a child's parents don't live together, the parent who lives with the child provides his or her daily care. The parent who doesn't live with the child is required by law to provide money to help take care of the child. This payment is called child support.) Calvin will be released next year. How much money he pays Kerry for Vanessa's care will depend on whether he works and how much money he earns.

According to Joanne Bednar, who has worked for 20 years at a community health care clinic that provides medical and counseling services to teenage mothers, many unmarried teenage mothers do not receive financial support from the fathers. "At most, it's a box of diapers on occasion or an outfit for a special event," she says.

"Some of the fathers are supportive during the pregnancy," Bednar continues, "but right around the time the baby is born, they start to feel the responsibility and walk out."

More than a million teenage girls become pregnant each year in the United States. Although the situation is different for each of them, research shows that most are not married.

The consequences of "going it alone" are far-reaching, as Kerry and many teenage mothers like her know. It can be a struggle to make ends meet each month. There are the basic expenses of food, rent, electricity, telephone, transportation, and medical insurance for both mother and child. These add up to $1,000 a month or more. The mother must also buy many other items for the baby, such as a crib, stroller, car seat, formula, diapers, clothes—and the list goes on. These additional expenses can total another $1,000 a month or more.

Kerry's boyfriend, Bill, helps take care of Vanessa.

In many ways, Kerry is lucky. She benefits from a number of social programs available where she lives, in Minneapolis. She receives free day care (while she attends school during the day), free milk for her and Vanessa, food stamps to help buy groceries, and a welfare check for $437 each month. (Welfare payments are administered by the Welfare Department, a government agency that assists low-income people.)

But even with this assistance, Kerry says that it is difficult to get by. Her basic monthly expenses are $360 for rent, about $15 for electricity, and $30 for telephone, for a total of $405. That's not counting expenses for things like diapers, the deposit she paid on her apartment, clothes for her and Vanessa, and so on. The $437 she receives from welfare is gone three days after she gets it. Luckily, Kerry's boyfriend, Bill, helps out by paying just about all of the bills except rent. Even so, Kerry has to rely on charge cards to buy necessities like diapers.

Kerry would like to get off welfare. "I'd rather work," she says. "You know, me being on welfare is kind of weird. Nobody in my family is on welfare. I wasn't raised that way....I want to make it on my own."

Getting from one place to another with a toddler can take extra time.

She hopes to get a job and finish school at night. This might not be a realistic solution, however. If Kerry gets a full-time job while trying to finish school, she'll have little or no time to spend with her daughter, and she will have to find—and pay—someone to babysit Vanessa. She'll also have to deal with the stress of trying to do three things well at once—parent, study, and work.

What's more, if Kerry decides to quit school and work full-time, she will also lose her welfare payment and the free day care for Vanessa. To make up for the loss of government assistance, she would have to find a very high-paying job. The reality is that most people her age—whether or not they are parents—work at jobs that pay the minimum wage or close to it.

Some teenage mothers create a more workable situation with the help of their families. This is true particularly for girls from cultures in which large extended families are common, such as Southeast Asian and Native American. According to Rita LaChapelle, a nurse who works with teen mothers, these cultures are often supportive of teenage pregnancies. With family support, the teenage mother may be able to live at home and take advantage of built-in babysitters—an extremely important form of support if the mother hopes to finish high school.

Kerry and Vanessa have fun at a family birthday party. Kerry's family helps ease the burden of caring for a baby.

While she was pregnant, Kerry lived with her grandmother, then with her cousin. Toward the end of her pregnancy, she rented an apartment of her own. "I didn't know if I was going to be able to get a phone right away or not," Kerry recalls, "and I didn't have very much furniture. Even though Bill was coming over quite a bit, there were times when I got scared. It's a lot better living with him now, even though all of the other things—like money—can still be pretty scary sometimes."

Kerry's grandmother on her mom's side of the family has been supportive of Kerry and Vanessa.

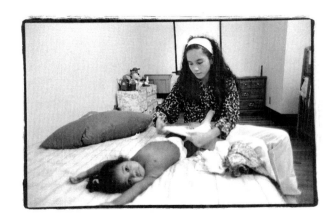

Just before leaving the apartment for the day-care center, Kerry discovers that Vanessa's diaper is dirty and has to be changed. In the bedroom, where the diapers are kept, the yellowing shades are pulled down to block out the hot sun. Vanessa's toys are in one corner of the room—busy beads and a little swing set with Sesame Street characters rocking slowly back and forth on it. In another corner are a jigsaw puzzle and the game of Life, which help Kerry fill the many hours she spends at home in the evenings when Vanessa is sleeping.

Vanessa wiggles and fights as Kerry struggles to get the diaper securely in place. Kerry says Vanessa has been going through a phase lately. Like most babies her age, she wants to have more control over her world. This often translates into temper tantrums, complete with hitting and biting. It was much easier when Vanessa was an infant, Kerry says, when almost all she did was sleep.

After tossing the dirty diaper into an overflowing diaper pail and washing her hands, Kerry throws the bag of baby things over her shoulder, scoops Vanessa up onto one hip, and balances the car seat on the other. She's thankful that she only has to walk down one flight of stairs to get to the street.

On the narrow street, cars are parked bumper to bumper, and the buildings stand just a step or two off the sidewalks. For the most part, this neighborhood isn't a place where people stay long. Like many other tenants in her building, Kerry hopes to find another place to live soon. But, for right now, it's all she can afford.

The day-care center is a modern building with air-conditioning, new cribs, and lots of toys. The sun pours through a wall of windows into the children's play area. Vanessa runs to one of the younger babies and tries to kiss her, but the baby wants no part of it and pushes Vanessa away. Vanessa suddenly catches her reflection in one of the mirrors and jumps up and down, giggling.

Through a county program, Kerry receives free day care as long as she is in school. She's glad, because her high school doesn't offer day-care services. Kerry's also lucky that county funds are available for the program right now. Lisa Peterson, who runs the day-care center, says that while the day-care program helps a lot of people, "it's certainly not something that parents can automatically count on. Money [for the program] may be there one year and gone the next."

Single parenting is difficult, especially for teens, according to Peterson, but Kerry is unusual in many ways. "She takes the time to do things, like bake a cake for her daughter's birthday party here," Peterson says. "For many single teen mothers, it's more than they can handle just getting their child here, getting themselves to school, and picking their children up again at night.... Many of them want to be more involved, but they just don't have the energy and time to do it.

"It's a constant struggle being a single parent," Peterson continues. "Just the day-to-day stuff, like going to the grocery store with the baby rather than being able to leave the child with someone. It takes a lot more out of you."

According to Peterson, Kerry is very responsible. For instance, unlike many young parents, Kerry recognizes when Vanessa has an illness that won't go away by itself and needs to see a doctor.

"We've seen other parents who haven't done such a good job because they're so overwhelmed by all of the responsibility," says Peterson.

One reason Kerry seems to be coping better than many teen parents is that she has accepted the responsibility that goes along with parenting. She is determined not to give up, no matter what it takes. Accepting that responsibility, however, has meant making a lot of changes in her life.

"Before Vanessa was born, I went out a lot with my friends," Kerry says. "I still try to get out, but now it's once in a blue moon. Having Vanessa forced me to settle down because of the responsibility and the fact that I really need to get my schooling done.... That means not going out as much as you want, spending money on your child instead of yourself, and feeding her first even if you're starving."

Staying home doesn't bother Kerry too much, though, mainly because she's exhausted by the end of the day. She starts each day at about 7:00 A.M. and doesn't usually go to sleep until about 1:00 A.M.

What little free time Kerry has she spends in various ways: attending a parenting class once a week at her school, participating in events at the day-care center with Vanessa, going to Native American powwows with her mother and Vanessa, and taking Vanessa to a nearby lake to feed the ducks—one of Vanessa's favorite activities.

Kerry also spends a lot of time tracking down resources that will help her and Vanessa—medical assistance, welfare, possibilities for subsidized housing, and so on. She has spent many hours finding the right programs and filling out the necessary forms.

Some teen parents are unable or unwilling to make changes in their lifestyle. They want to continue on as before—doing things with their friends instead of tending to the needs of the child. The child might go without proper meals, naps, and baths.

Kerry must fill out many forms to receive the public assistance she needs to survive as a single mother.

In other cases, the teen parent simply gives up, as Kerry has seen some of her friends do. Many of these girls have quit school. They can't take very good care of their children, because they're so overwhelmed by the financial, emotional, and physical obstacles they face.

"I've tried to help some of my other friends with kids get into the [day-care] program and stuff, but they don't want to do anything about it," says Kerry. "It's too much work, or they figure they're not going to get in. So they quit school and just stay home and stay stuck."

While it's not easy to take care of an infant, most parents agree that raising children gets harder—not easier—as time goes on. Counselor Joanne Bednar comments, "The responsibility of being a parent often doesn't really hit young mothers until the baby starts moving around and testing limits at about the age of nine months. That's when we start seeing a number of discipline problems with the kids. For example, the young parent may not know how to give positive reinforcement to the child, so the only time the child gets attention is when he or she is bad and gets yelled at. The child learns that the only way to get attention is to do more negative things, and the mother gets increasingly frustrated."

So far, Kerry's experience with Vanessa follows this pattern. "At first, it was pretty easy because all Vanessa did was sleep," Kerry says. "Although sometimes she'd start crying, and it would really get to me. Now the hardest part is disciplining her. I tell her 'no,' but sometimes I let her get away with whatever she's doing when I know I shouldn't. It's teaching her that she doesn't have to listen to me when I say no."

In spite of the difficulties, sacrifices, and responsibility, the job of parenting has some rewards for Kerry. "What I like best is doing things with Vanessa," she says. "I love to see her enjoy herself, laugh and smile and have fun. Every once in a while she'll come over to me and give me a hug and a kiss. She makes this cute smacking sound with her mouth. It's the little things like that that keep you going."

It's almost 8:45 A.M., and Kerry has to hurry. She's going to school this summer, and classes begin at 9:00. Luckily, her ride waited for her while she dropped Vanessa off, and she should make it just in time.

When Kerry enters the school building this morning, she immediately heads for the stairs. She hates being confined in small places such as elevators. That's why, during her sixth month of pregnancy, in her sophomore year, Kerry quit school. With the added weight she was carrying, she couldn't manage the five flights of stairs that led to her classrooms.

At that point, Kerry was already a year behind in school, having changed schools and homes three times the year before she became pregnant. With each move, she fell further behind in her schoolwork and lost credits.

Kerry's current school is an alternative school for students 16 years of age or older who, like Kerry, have fallen behind for one reason or another. The school is set up to allow students to obtain not only a high school diploma, but also two years of university or technical college credit—free of charge.

Unlike regular schools, which usually start classes at 7:20 A.M., class hours at Kerry's school are noon to 5:00 P.M. during the school year and 9:00 to 5:00 during the summer. Ron Eikkas, a counselor at the school, says, "We have a lot of girls, like Kerry, who need to take care of their kids and get them to day care in the morning, which is almost impossible to do while attending a regular school."

Students are also allowed to work at their own pace. At most schools, a student automatically fails after 10 days' absence. Kerry's school only pays attention to the days a student is there. "That way," Eikkas says, "a student isn't penalized for having a sick child, a problem with day care, or any other personal problems that force them to miss school."

Kerry is anxious to finish high school and go to college. She's considering a college in River Falls, Wisconsin, not only because many of her friends go there, but also because the school offers a number of financial aid grants.

"It's Vanessa who got me motivated," Kerry says. "Because of her, I want to be something. I don't want to be on welfare the rest of my life. Without my schooling, I wouldn't get anywhere. I could probably get a job, but not making what I could if I go on to school."

Kerry isn't exactly sure what she wants to do for a career, but she does know what she likes. Her favorite subjects at school are psychology and English, and she knows she wants to work with kids. Right now, she's thinking about the possibility of becoming a teacher, a child psychologist, or a parole officer for juveniles.

Kerry's ability to look ahead and plan for the future is exceptional. "As hard as they try, most teenage mothers drop out and very few ever go on to college," says Joanne Bednar. "For many of the girls, it just doesn't seem to matter—they're living one day at a time and not looking ahead. I asked one young mother what her goals were for the future, and she didn't seem to know what I was talking about. Life went on from one day to the next, without ever planning ahead. And the younger they are, the worse it seems to be. As these girls get a little bit older, however, they begin to develop better problem-solving skills and realize that they need to look beyond today."

Other goals Kerry hopes to achieve include having one or two more children, owning a house and a car, and perhaps someday having someone there—a husband—to help out.

Sitting in front of a computer in the computer lab, Kerry finishes an assignment for her economics class. A teacher stands nearby to help students with questions, but for the most part Kerry works independently. She won't have time to start her assignments for her other two classes—government and psychology—because it's almost 2:00 P.M. Vanessa's 15-month checkup at the doctor's office is at 3:00, and it will take an hour to get there by bus.

Kerry shuts off the computer, packs up her belongings, and hurries down the front steps of her school toward the day care. Vanessa is a little crabby when Kerry rouses her from her nap, but she's happy to see her mom. Luckily, she dozes for most of the bus ride to the clinic. When they get off the bus, Vanessa comes to life. She runs through the grass and squeals in delight at all the "birdies" flying overhead.

Vanessa doesn't want to go in the medical building and begins to cry as Kerry grabs her hand and leads her inside. In the reception area, Kerry quickly picks up a magazine and begins reading to her child. It works. Vanessa stops crying, fascinated by the pictures of frogs that Kerry points out.

A few minutes later, the nurse calls Vanessa's name, and Kerry and Vanessa follow her to the examining room. The look in Vanessa's eyes the minute they enter the room seems to say, "A whole new place to explore!" She pulls diapers off the medical cart, looks in the drawers underneath the examining table, and digs through the medical supplies she finds there. A blood pressure tube becomes her favorite "toy."

"Not in your mouth!" Kerry tells her, and Vanessa obeys.

Today Vanessa will receive the last of her DPT (diphtheria, pertussis, and tetanus) shots until she's five years old. She also has to have an MMR (measles, mumps, rubella) shot and a blood test to check for iron.

For now, tending to Vanessa's checkups and illnesses, which have included colds, flu, diarrhea, and several ear infections, hasn't been much of a problem for Kerry—except the sleepless nights she spends whenever Vanessa is sick. All of Kerry's and Vanessa's medical expenses are covered by Kerry's mother's insurance policy. But that only lasts until Kerry is 21 and out of school.

After the nurse has updated Vanessa's medical record, Vanessa's doctor comes in. She discusses summer safety concerns with Kerry—how to prevent sunburn, safety around swimming pools, and the need for car seats. She asks if Kerry has any ipecac syrup on hand in case Vanessa ever drinks or eats something poisonous. The ipecac syrup will help make Vanessa vomit and get rid of the poison. Kerry says no, so Dr. Liebo promises to give her some before she leaves.

The doctor checks Vanessa's ears.

Dr. Liebo then asks Kerry about Vanessa's speech, eating habits, sleeping patterns, and day-care arrangements, to make sure that Vanessa is developing as she should and that she's being well cared for. In the middle of all the questions and answers, Vanessa slams her hand in a drawer. Kerry calmly kisses the pain away, and Vanessa's tears disappear.

Dr. Liebo learns that Vanessa is still drinking from a bottle at 15 months and instructs Kerry to get rid of the bottles. "Children should be drinking from a cup at 12 months," she says. She also gives Kerry some information on potty training for future reference.

Dr. Liebo leaves to get the ipecac syrup. For the moment, Vanessa is staying out of trouble, and Kerry starts to daydream. She remembers a time when she was in another examining room, two years ago.

"The test is positive," the doctor told her then. "You're about eight weeks pregnant."

Kerry's first reaction was disbelief. It took her a couple of days to get over the shock. "I felt like I was too young to have a baby," she says. "I wasn't done with school yet. But I didn't go through a lot of confusion about what to do. I knew I was going to keep her and make the best of it."

That day, Kerry became one of more than one million teenage girls who become pregnant each year in the United States. According to the Alan Guttmacher Institute, by age 18, one in four teenage girls will become pregnant. The United States has one of the highest rates of teenage pregnancy in the Western world.

Not everyone who becomes pregnant opts to go through with the pregnancy or keep the baby after it is born, however. In 1989, only about half of all teenage pregnancies resulted in birth; 37 percent ended in abortion and about 14 percent in miscarriage. Less than 10 percent of teenagers who give birth place their babies for adoption.

Research also shows that 8 out of 10 teenage pregnancies in the United States are unintended (9 in 10 among unmarried teenagers and about half among married teenagers). Such was the case with Kerry. "I guess I just wasn't thinking," she says. "I figured it could never happen to me, because I didn't use birth control in the past and I never got pregnant. I had the pill, but I never took it because it made me sick, like I'd have to throw up or something—and who wants to feel that way every day?"

Kerry beat the odds by not getting pregnant sooner. According to one study, half of all teenage mothers became pregnant within six months of their first experience of intercourse.

When teenage mothers are interviewed, they give a number of explanations of why they ended up pregnant unintentionally. Like Kerry, many girls say the pill made them sick, so they didn't take it. Other reasons include:

- They wanted to hang on to their boyfriends and thought sex was a way to do that
- They wanted their boyfriends or a baby to love them
- Being sexually active makes you popular
- Their parents were gone a lot, and they wanted to be with someone
- They were just living for the moment and not thinking about tomorrow

The most common response, however, is like Kerry's—"I never thought it would happen to me."

Many teens believe they can't get pregnant the first time they have sex. Part of the reason for this may stem from the impact of watching television. According to a recent report in *TV Guide,* "In an average year, American television viewers are exposed to some 9,230 scenes of suggested sexual intercourse or innuendo and fully 94 percent of the sex on soap operas involves people not married to each other. In the exciting and glamorized sex of movieland, videoland, and rock-musicland, no one uses contraceptives, and hardly anyone gets pregnant."

For many girls, when the doctor or home pregnancy test confirmed that they were pregnant, they felt sad. They were scared and worried—not only about having to tell their parents and friends, but about having to cope with the enormous responsibility that faced them. In the matter of seconds it takes to confirm a pregnancy, a girl's entire life changes.

Most girls felt they had made a mistake—they hadn't planned to become pregnant—but it was difficult to think about giving up the baby through adoption or abortion. Instead, they accepted the consequences. For many teenage mothers, this means living on welfare, dropping out of school, and perhaps worst of all, losing what remained of their own childhoods. If they had it to do over again, most would try not to get pregnant in the first place.

Not all pregnancies among teenagers are unplanned, however. Some teenage parents plan a pregnancy. Some think that having a baby will be a way to get away from home, or they mistakenly believe that the public assistance they will receive if they have a child will allow them to finance their "escape."

Others see becoming a parent as a quick route to becoming an adult. Still others don't like school or the thought of working, and they see having a child as an acceptable alternative.

Finally, there are those who simply want to feel like they have some control over their lives; a baby is something no one can take away from them.

"You think they're cute, huggable, lovable babies that wear little itty-bitty baby shoes and T-shirts," said one young mother who was interviewed for a video on teenage parenting. "What you don't know is that it takes a lot of money...and it's a full-time, all-day job."

Joanne Bednar observes that many teenage girls are up-front about saying they want to be pregnant. "But when you tell them their pregnancy test is positive, they break into tears," she says. "They're scared to death. They're just kids."

Kerry remembers what it was like to have to tell her mother that she was pregnant. She chose to do it without words—she just handed her mother the slip of paper she received from the Public Health Department saying she was eight weeks pregnant.

"My mom and I were always close, but we weren't during that time," Kerry recalls. "I don't know if it was because of the pregnancy or because of the guy she was dating, but it was different then."

Kerry and her mother have been through some ups and downs since Kerry became pregnant.

As for Kerry's father, he didn't find out until the day after Vanessa was born.

"My mom called him from the hospital and told him," Kerry says. "He came up the next day and brought me a bumper set to go with my crib and a lot of little T-shirts and a nice little knitted sweater. He accepted her, but he didn't tell his two other kids about Vanessa until six months ago. Until then, they didn't even know she was alive."

What hurt Kerry the most was the reaction from her grandmother on her dad's side of the family. "We were always so close," Kerry says. "My grandmother lives on the Lower East Side in New York, and I used to go out there every summer. Even though I was the oldest grandchild in the family, I was always her baby."

Kerry was afraid to tell her grandmother about Vanessa. "Even after Vanessa was born, I thought about leaving her with my mom and just going to New York to visit like nothing had happened," Kerry says. "But my dad told her, and my grandmother hasn't talked to me since. That's really hurt me."

Kerry isn't sure why her grandmother won't accept Vanessa. "I don't know," she says. "Maybe my grandma was just disappointed that I got pregnant so young. Maybe she just had higher hopes for me."

Kerry's family includes her daughter, her mother, and her mother's mother.

43

It's 10:00 P.M. Vanessa is fed, bathed, diapered, and asleep in her crib—at last. Kerry has a little time to get the apartment cleaned up, do some schoolwork, wash clothes and dishes, and get ready for tomorrow, when she'll start the same routine over again.

She takes a minute to think about the day. Did she get everything done? Is there anything she forgot? She stares out the window to the now dark and empty street. She speaks about all the things she wants for Vanessa.

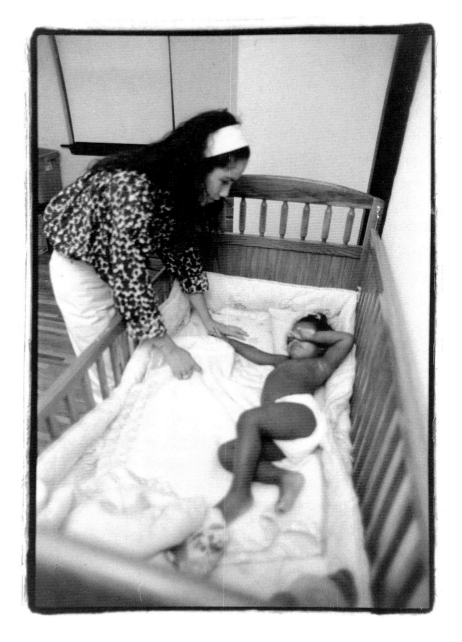

"I want her to stay in school and finish," she says. "I want her to go to college and make something of herself. And I want to teach her to respect people. Vanessa can be so mean at times and push or slap the other kids. Maybe it's typical for her age, but I don't like it.

"I really hope Vanessa doesn't get pregnant young, like I did," Kerry adds. "I would hate to see her go through everything I have to go through. Down the road, I'm going to take steps to make sure that doesn't happen. I'm going to make sure she's on birth control."

If Vanessa did get pregnant in her teens, Kerry says, "I'd probably be upset at first, but I'd be supportive about whatever she wanted to do. I'd make sure she knew the facts. I'd tell her that it's harder than you think to raise a child—much harder. It's hard going to school with a child, it's hard taking the bottle away, it's hard getting the child to listen.

"I'd tell her about all of the times she, as a baby, was running a fever during the night and how I'd sit up with her, not knowing what was the matter or what to do. I'd tell her about having to change all my plans at the last minute—not go to school—because I needed to take her to the doctor. I'd tell her that facing a child 24 hours a day is hard work, and there's not much left over for anything else.

"But if she decided to have the baby, I'd make sure and tell her the most important thing of all—not to give up hope. That's the biggest danger. There are people at my school who have gone through the toughest lives you can imagine, and they're pulling out of it and are going to make it. No matter what happens to you in life, you can still become the person and have the life you really want if you're willing to work hard."

For Further Reading

Arthur, Shirley. *Surviving Teen Pregnancy: Your Choices, Dreams, and Decisions.* Buena Park, CA: Morning Glory Press, 1991.

Beyer, Kay. *Coping with Teen Parenting.* New York: Rosen Publishing Group, 1990.

Bode, Janet. *Kids Having Kids: The Unwed Teenage Parent.* New York: Franklin Watts, 1980.

Bowe-Gutman, Sonia. *Teen Pregnancy.* Minneapolis: Lerner Publications, 1987.

Kuklin, Susan. *What Do I Do Now? Talking about Teenage Pregnancy.* New York: Putnams, 1991.

Lindsay, Jeanne Warren, and Jean Brunelli. *Your Pregnancy and Newborn Journey: How to Take Care of Yourself and Your Newborn If You're a Pregnant Teen.* Buena Park, CA: Morning Glory Press, 1992.

Meier, Gisela. *Teenage Pregnancy.* New York: Marshall Cavendish, 1994.

Silverstein, Herma. *Teen Guide to Single Parenting.* New York: Franklin Watts, 1989.

Simpson, Carolyn. *Coping with an Unplanned Pregnancy.* New York: Rosen Publishing Group, 1990.

Sources for the statistics cited in this book include: "Facts in Brief," published by the Alan Guttmacher Institute, Washington, D.C., 1993; "A State-by-State Look at Teenage Childbearing in the U.S.," published by the Charles Stewart Mott Foundation, 1991; and "Counseling Adolescents with Problem Pregnancies," by Jeanne Marecek, Swarthmore College, published in *American Psychologist* (January 1987).